EDEN
VALLEY
WALK

Kent
County
Council
PLANNING

EDEN

VALLEY

WALK

Discover the many faces of Kent

Designed and produced by
Countryside Group and County Visuals,
Kent County Council
Planning Department.

Text edited by Caroline Wing.
Illustrations by John Cann.

Maps produced by County Visuals,
with the sanction of the controller of
HM Stationery Office,
Crown copyright reserved.

Printed in Great Britain by
Alcris Ltd,
Unit 4, Chapel Park,
Church Road Business Centre,
Murston, Sittingbourne,
Kent ME10 3RS

Published by Kent County Council,
Planning Department,
Springfield, Maidstone, Kent
ME14 2LX,
with assistance from the
Countryside Commission.

First published April 1991.

ISBN 1 873010 06 0

CONTENTS

To the best of our knowledge the historical content and all other information is believed to be correct. We would be grateful if you would inform us of any changes, omissions or errors, so that modifications can be made in subsequent revisions of the book.

HIGH WEALD
An Area of Outstanding Natural Beauty (AONB)

The term 'Weald' is given to the area between the Greensand belts to the north and south. The sandstones and clays of the exposed centre of the Wealden dome, the 'High Weald' give rise to a hilly, broken and remote country of ridges and valleys. In contrast, open areas of the AONB include Ashdown Forest and to the north and east, rich landscapes of historical parkland, orchards and hopfields. The AONB meets the coast at Hastings.

A close patchwork of small fields, hedges and woods patterns the rolling landscape, which is characterised by its distinctive brick, tile-hung and white weatherboard houses, its oasthouses and also by the traces of the ancient Wealden iron industry such as hammer ponds.

The dense forest that gave the Weald its name (derived from the German word 'Wold') has largely vanished but fine ancient broadleaved woodland is still abundant particularly in the deep ravines that cut into ridges.

Agriculture is central to the rural economy: dairying, mixed farming and horticulture, with a current trend towards cereals. Forestry and mineral extraction remain traditional Wealden industries. There are no major settlements but the major growth of adjacent urban areas such as Tunbridge Wells has resulted in a high proportion of commuter population in the AONB villages.

RIVER MEDWAY

The River Medway is the largest river in the Southern Region of the National Rivers Authority.

Course and Geology

The river rises in the Ashdown Forest as a spring issuing from the Tunbridge Wells Sands just above Turners Hill. The sands and clays of the High Weald which underlie the Upper Medway dictate the character of the river. With its many deeply incised tributaries, the river contrasts sharply with the chalk streams found in other parts of the region. The Wealden clays are impermeable to rainfall and water finds its way across the surface of the steeply sloping land creating a multitude of small rushing streams.

Tiny streams in deep V valleys meet to form a typical Wealden vale as the river flows north-eastwards towards Penshurst. There, the river is joined by the River Eden and at Ensfield the river valley opens out where High and Low Weald meet. As the river flows across the Vale of Kent, the valley is less steep though the river still collects tributaries which have their origins in other parts of the High Weald. The Medway cuts its way through the Greensand Ridge beyond Yalding before reaching the County Town of Maidstone.

Allington Lock forms the tidal limit of the Medway in Maidstone from whence the river flows north, cutting through the chalk. The estuary widens between Rochester and Sheerness where the River Medway flows into the Thames Estuary.

History

The name of the river derives from a Celtic word Medu, meaning mead, presumably signifying a river with 'sweet' water. The Romans called the river Fluminus Meduwaeias and the Saxons knew it as the Medwaeg.

The importance of the area to the Romans lay in the relatively rich and accessible iron deposits of the area which had first been exploited on a small scale in the Iron Age. The grey Wadhurst clay contains iron nodules or 'sows', some with iron contents as high as 55%. The Weald was one of the largest areas of iron making in Europe for nearly two centuries, producing many thousands of tons of iron. The Romans used the bloomery process for smelting iron. The ore was heated by charcoal in a clay-walled mound through which air was forced by bellows. The forest of the Ashdown Sands and the High Weald supplied abundant timber to fuel the process. The industry fell into decline but revived again in Tudor times when the more sophisticated blast furnaces were introduced by the French and pioneered on the headstreams of the Medway. The process produced cast iron which could then be forged into wrought iron. The bellows for supplying the furnace and the trip hammers for forging the iron needed power. The steep Wealden streams proved ideal for impounding as 'furnace' or 'hammer' ponds to provide a head of water to drive the twin waterwheels characteristic of Tudor forges.

Flood Defence

The Medway and its tributaries respond very quickly to rainfall, especially in winter. The impermeable clay and large areas of urban development result in a rapid run-off. For this reason, the National Rivers Authority's Flood Defence role is of paramount importance.

Historically the Medway and Eden Valleys had suffered flooding of both agricultural land and property. In 1968 the worst recorded flood in living memory occurred causing massive damage both in the town of Tonbridge and in the downstream areas. In order to alleviate flooding, a flood storage area with flood control gates was constructed above Tonbridge at Leigh and is now operated by the NRA. This is the largest on-river flood storage area in the United Kingdom.

In times of heavy rainfall three gates in an earthen embankment across the river regulate the amount of flood water passing downstream to Tonbridge.

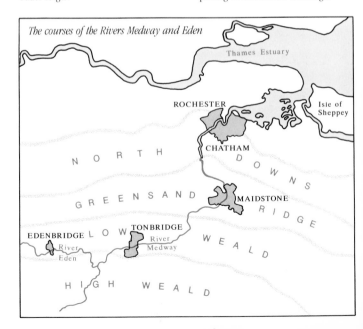

The courses of the Rivers Medway and Eden

Farmland at Lydens Farm, near Hever

Some of the run-off is held back, forming a temporary lake, whenever the flows exceed the channel capacities through the town. The 'lake' can later be drained at a controlled rate once flood flows have abated.

EDEN VALLEY

The River Eden rises in Surrey and flows south-east for about 15 miles until reaching the River Medway at Penshurst where the combined water courses meander on to Tonbridge, Maidstone and eventually the Thames Estuary. From Edenbridge to Tonbridge the valley runs between the undulating High Weald to the south and the comparatively flat and wet clayland of the Low Weald and the Greensand Ridge to the north.

Natural History

There is considerable wildlife interest in the picturesque Eden valley. Small pockets of wet meadowland, woodland and undisturbed river bank have survived modern farming practices and these support some rare plant and animal species.

The river flows through the Wealden Clay flood plain and cuts through gravel deposits below Hever Castle and between Leigh and Penshurst there are steep cliffs of Tunbridge Wells sand. The flow varies considerably according to the season, and has in the past resulted in serious flooding of Tonbridge. This threat has now been removed by construction of the Leigh flood barrier.

The Weald of Kent once had extensive stretches of species-rich woodland and a few areas remain within the Eden valley - to the south of Chiddingstone, for example. Bird watching can be most rewarding, especially where there is a mixture of farmland, hedgerow, woodland and river. Green woodpecker, kestrel, kingfisher and heron may be seen. During the summer the occasional hobby and different kinds of warblers may visit and winter brings other residents such as ducks, lapwings, snipe, redwing and fieldfare.

Aquatic and marginal plants to be found in and beside the river include broadleaved pond weed, yellow water lily, simple and branched bur-reed, water plantain and water chickweed. There is a wide range of sedges including some rare species and purple

and yellow loosestrifes occur on the margins.

The river, and lakes through which it flows, provides homes for many invertebrates. Dragonflies are numerous including the emperor dragonfly and banded damselfly. The rivers form a major stronghold in the British Isles for the white-legged damselfly. Other water animals include frogs, grass snakes, water voles and the rather less welcome introduced mink. Mammals such as stoat, weasel, wood mouse and bank vole occur nearby.

Archaeology and History

Some limited evidence has been found for the Old and Middle Stone Age hunter-gatherers who ranged across this, once post-glacial landscape. Flint implements abandoned by these peoples are found along the valley but less is known about their temporary camps. Excavation of a rock shelter at Stonewell near Chiddingstone exposed a charred 'occupation' layer and the remains of some burnt hazelnuts, and three further, potentially inhabited, rock shelters have been located in the Penshurst area. With gradual improvement in the climate the deciduous woods of the Weald grew

increasingly dense and the paucity of archaeological finds suggest that by the New Stone Age, communities visited the woods only occasionally.

Towards the end of the 1st millennium BC late Iron Age communities started to exploit the iron ore deposits held within Wealden sandstone and iron smelting has been recorded during archaeological excavations at Dry Hill fort. The fort which sits on a high and circular hilltop to the south-west of Edenbridge covers an area of 24 acres and is enclosed by a series of three earthen ramparts.

The iron smelting site located just to the south of Dry Hill may date to the Roman period. North-south roadways constructed across this area would have helped to stimulate a developing iron industry and that running through what is now the centre of Edenbridge provided a river crossing for the main north-south link. Roman pottery and slag found near Chiddingstone Hoath demonstrate that industrial activity could occur several miles from the main roadway.

By the late 11th century the major route was that which ran from Rochester and Wrotham to Lewes and Pevensey. The road crossed the River Medway at Tonbridge and there is little doubt that the first stone bridge across the river here was built at the same time as the castle guarding it, soon after the Norman invasion. During the 13th century Tonbridge continued to flourish with the castle protecting the 'Great Bridge' over which ran what was now the most important route, that from London and Sevenoaks to Lamberhurst, Rye and Hastings; but in the 14th century other crossing points of the rivers were improved. The countryside around contained several wealthy estates. Some of the richer residences were embellished and fortified, Penshurst Place receiving a licence to crenellate in 1341, and Hever Castle in 1384. Additionally several moated manorial sites are to be found close to the walk: these prestigious sites, which were typically constructed between 1250 and 1350, are useful indicators of the distribution of rural wealth and status in the medieval period.

From this time and into the post-medieval period, whilst the area was still quite thickly wooded, the Wealden iron industry underwent considerable rejuvenation. Six separate iron industry sites are known within a couple of miles of the walk but what remains of these varies greatly. The industry was water powered and the traces of substantial water management systems sometime survive; remains of a large artificial pond, a so-called *pond bay* can be seen to the north of Hever. Rather less tangible, however, are the spreads of slag found west of Leigh and a short distance from the railway south-west of Hever. Some other sites are only known from documentary sources.

In 1740 an Upper Medway Navigation Act was passed, allowing the whole of the river to be made navigable and by the early 19th century a spacious wharf had been created just below the bridge at Tonbridge. Upstream from here, however, the work was never completed, though digging of new canals for the Penshurst Canal Company was started in 1829. Only the 'Long Reach' and 'Straight Mile' were built. The latter, which is cut through by the Haysden Water and the Tonbridge bypass, has long been dry.

A direct railway line, running west from Tonbridge was built in 1842, linking this now prosperous area to Redhill. This was the original London to Dover Line via Edenbridge.

View of Penshurst Village from the bridge

The design of the Eden Valley Walk logo is an artistic representation of the four main elements of the valley through which the route passes; the river, bridges, historic buildings and countryside.

WALKING ADVICE

No season of the year is closed to walkers; enjoyment can be gained from walking on a bright crisp winter's morning, or on an 'Indian summer's day' in the autumn. Equally rewarding is a springtime walk when the countryside is full of new life and growth.

Be prepared for cold and wet weather. Take with you clothes which are warm and waterproof. Sections of the path may be muddy after periods of rain so wear strong, comfortable and, waterproof footwear. Inexpensive overtrousers will protect you from any discomfort caused by walking through high vegetation after rain. In case you come across a path which has become overgrown, you would find it useful to carry secateurs to help clear the way. Take care when crossing or walking along country roads.

Reckon on walking 2 or 2½" miles an hour. However, the distances and time for the walk are shown on the route maps, and in the information. Allow more time if it has been wet, if you are elderly or have children or inexperienced walkers with you.

The route has been established in consultation with landowners and follows public rights of way.

Please remember that most of the public paths cross private estates and farmland.

You are walking through a place of work; enjoy the countryside but please show respect and consideration for its life and work.

Remember to leave things as they are - fasten those gates you find closed and take your litter home with you otherwise it can injure people and animals (including wildlife). Guard against all risk of fire, especially in dry weather. Picnicking is not permitted on private land.

Dogs should be under control at all times, if not on a lead they can run surprisingly long distances in a short time and cause distress to people and animals not in the immediate vicinity and therefore out of sight of the owner. Farmers have a right to shoot dogs found worrying animals. Walkers are particularly requested to keep their dogs on leads at all times in Penshurst Park.

Footpaths are for people on foot only, remember to always use gates and stiles to cross fences and hedges. If the path goes through a growing crop please walk in single file. Paths were mostly developed as routes from farms to the nearest village and so were not designed for large numbers of walkers.

Please leave wild flowers for others to enjoy. Remember that crops and animals are the farmers' livelihood so please leave them alone.

USING THE GUIDEBOOK

Although it is possible to walk the route of the Eden Valley Walk in either direction, the maps have been arranged in sequence in three sections from Cernes Farm (Haxted Mill) to Tonbridge.

ROUTE MAP INFORMATION

The route maps are reproduced from the Ordnance Survey 1:10,000 series.

The maps are aligned north/south on each page, and run from west to east throughout the book. The scale appears on each map spread.

MAPS

Ordnance Survey sheet numbers and titles.

Landranger Series, scale 1:50,000-1¼" to the mile.
187 Dorking, Reigate and Crawley area
188 Maidstone and The Weald of Kent

Pathfinder Series, scale 1:25,000-2½" to the mile.
1228 (TQ 44/54) Tonbridge and Edenbridge.

DISTANCES AND TIME

The distances and times for each section of the walk are shown on the map spreads or in the information below.

PLANNING A WALK

This walk has been developed with regard to the rail and road communications which will enable you to return conveniently to your starting point.

The route is 15 miles in length and can be undertaken as a long distance walk in a day. Edenbridge, Hever, Leigh and Tonbridge are all easily reached by train from London and most parts of Kent, Surrey and East Sussex. Car parking is available at Haxted Mill for those wishing to start or finish at the Vanguard Way. Lingfield, with its railway station, is another suitable starting or finishing point.

If you wish to undertake the Eden Valley Walk in sections you need to be aware of problems of returning to your starting point. Possible solutions might be as follows:

a) using two cars, one at the starting point and the other at the proposed finishing point;

b) using one car and public transport. If relying on infrequent bus services it is suggested that you make your outward journey by bus thus returning confidently to your car or base;

c) retracing your steps - the scenery can look surprisingly different when you are walking the other way.

The walk can be undertaken in sections as follows:

Cernes Farm (Haxted Mill) - Edenbridge: 3 miles, allow 1½ hours.
Edenbridge - Hever (railway station): 3½ miles, allow 1¼ hours.
Hever (railway station) - Leigh (railway station): 6¾ miles, allow 3½ hours.
Leigh (village) - Tonbridge: 3½ miles, allow 1¼ hours.

Access for each of the above places is as follows:

Cernes Farm (Haxted Mill) - car only
Edenbridge - bus and train
Hever - bus and train
Leigh - bus and train
Tonbridge - bus and train

Please note:

The spur to and from Leigh is also an alternative route in the event of flooding in the valley below Killick's Bank. The route through Tonbridge Castle Grounds closes at sunset; alternatively use The Slade and Castle Street.

Henry VIII Public House, Hever

SIGNING AND WAYMARKING

The Eden Valley Walk logo and waymarks are used to show the line of the route; you will see them fixed to waymark posts, poles or the posts of gates or stiles. The Walk has been waymarked in such a way that it is possible for you to walk the route in either direction.

At regular points along the route you will see metal signs fixed to lamp posts or some other post. These show access to the route from towns, villages, railway stations and bus routes, and display the logo and arrow coloured brown and white.

These access points will enable you to devise your own shorter walks utilizing private and public transport.

Eden Valley Walk logo
(black logo on a yellow disc)

Linear waymark
(yellow arrow on a black disc)

Eden Valley Walk sign
(brown and white)

TRANSPORT

Car Parking

Car parking places are shown on the route maps. Please note that these are not necessarily car parks. If a car park is not available, please park thoughtfully and sensibly to avoid causing an obstruction or damaging roadside verges. Leave car securely locked with valuables out of sight.

We are grateful to the curator of Haxted Watermill and Museum, for granting permission for walkers to use the car park at Haxted Mill. Potential users are requested to park at the far end of the car park on the grass, leaving the area nearer the mill and restaurant free for their visitors.

Please note that at Hever the parking area opposite the church and King Henry VIII Inn is provided for the use of Hever Castle and Garden visitors, and King Henry VIII patrons only, and are not available to people walking the public footpaths generally and the Eden Valley Walk, in particular.

Bus Services

The table on the right shows bus routes to and around the Eden Valley Walk. For details of services please telephone the following enquiry offices:
Maidstone & District Motor Services (0634) 832666
Shearings Coach and Bus (0892) 24282
Kentish Bus and Coach Services (0474) 321300
East Surrey Buses (0342) 893080

Train Services

The following British Rail stations provide access to the Eden Valley Walk. For details of services (Table 148 for Edenbridge, Leigh and Tonbridge; Table 184 for Lingfield, Edenbridge Town and Hever), please telephone the information office, Tonbridge (0732) 770111. Please note that Penshurst Station is located at Chiddingstone Causeway.

Transport information is correct at the time of publication. You are advised to check details of your journey before travelling, particularly with respect to Sunday services.

Bus Services

Bus routes to and around the Eden Valley Walk

Service No.	Route	Days of Operation	Operator(s)
210	Tonbridge-Edenbridge	Mon-Sat	M&D
231	Tunbridge Wells-Edenbridge	Mon-Sat	M&D
232	Tunbridge Wells-Edenbridge	Sat	M&D
233	Tunbridge Wells-Edenbridge	Mon-Sat	M&D
234	Tunbridge Wells-Edenbridge	Mon-Fri	M&D/ES
236	Edenbridge-Holtye Common	Mon-Fri	ES
238	Brasted-Lingfield	Wed and Fri	ES

Selected services to Tonbridge

Service No.	From	Days of Operation	Operator
7/807	Maidstone/Tunbridge Wells	Daily	M&D
150	Chatham/Maidstone	Daily	SC
214	Tunbridge Wells	Mon-Sat	SC
215	Tunbridge Wells	Mon-Sat	M&D
222	Tunbridge Wells	Mon-Sat	M&D
454	Sevenoaks	Mon-Sat	KB
615/7	Tunbridge Wells	Sun	SC

Operators

M&D	Maidstone & District Motor Services
SC	Shearings Coach and Bus
KB	Kentish Bus and Coach Services
ES	East Surrey Buses as 'Kent Karrier' network

Bus routes are shown on the location map thus: | 210 |

USEFUL ADDRESSES AND/OR TELEPHONE NUMBERS

If you have any comments or suggestions about this or any other recreational route, please contact the Recreation Paths Officer, Planning Department, Kent County Council, Springfield, Maidstone, Kent ME14 2LX, tel: Maidstone (0622) 696168

The routes should not be obstructed in any way, but if they are please contact the Public Rights of Way Unit, Highways Department, Kent County Council, Springfield, Maidstone, Kent ME14 2LX, tel: Maidstone (0622) 696713

Weatherdial

(up-to-date weather forecast)
Inland Kent 0898 14 12

Tourist Information
 (including accommodation lists)

Edenbridge: Town Council Offices, Doggetts Barn, High Street, Edenbridge, Kent TN8 5AR, tel: Edenbridge (0732) 865368

Tonbridge: Tourist Information Centre, Castle Offices, Castle Street, Tonbridge, Kent, tel: Tonbridge (0732) 770929

The Ramblers

If having undertaken this walk, you find that walking really appeals to you, you may wish to consider joining the Ramblers, in which case please contact: The Ramblers' Association, 1/5 Wandsworth Road, London SW8 2XX, tel: 071 582 6878

ACCOMMODATION

Bed and Breakfast establishments are located in the following places: Edenbridge, Chiddingstone Causeway (2 miles), Penshurst and Tonbridge.

Please telephone the Tourist Information Centre in Tonbridge for details.

The Ramblers' Association (also listed) publishes the Ramblers Year Book which contains an accommodation list.

Youth Hostel: Crockham Hill (2¾ miles.)

Crockham Hill House, Crockham Hill, Edenbridge, Kent TN8 6RB, tel: Crockham Hill (0732) 866322

Please note that this hostel has restricted opening arrangements and may close during the currency of the guidebook.

Details of membership can be obtained from YHA National Office, Trevelyan House, 8 St Stephens Hill, St Albans, Herts AL1 2DY, tel: St Albans (0727) 55215. You may join the YHA on arrival at the hostel, but prior booking is advisable.

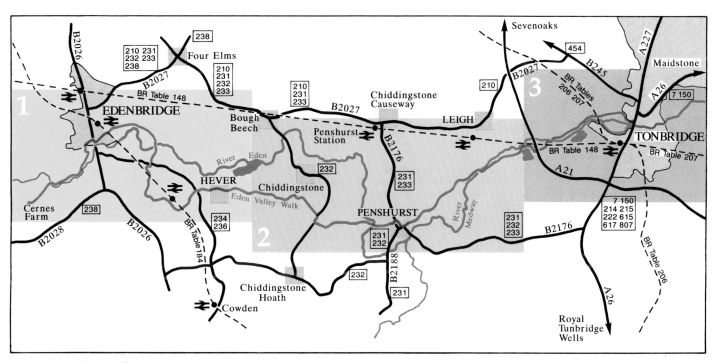

Location map, with details of bus and train services

Gateway, Penshurst Place

KEY TO MAP SYMBOLS

————	Eden Valley Walk - fully signed and waymarked
– – – –	Spur (access point) - fully signed and waymarked
· · · · ·	Optional access point or detour - not waymarked
24	Feature of interest
15	Miles from Cernes Farm
⇌	Railway station
🚌	Bus route
P	Car parking
☎	Telephone

i	Tourist Information
WC	Toilet
🛏	Accommodation
🍷	Public house
✕	Pub food
🍴	Cafe/restaurant
⊼	Picnic site
🛒	Foodstore
☀	Viewpoint
⚠	Caution - take care

1

Cernes Farm (Haxted Mill) - Threshers Field (Hever)
6 miles, allow 3 hours.

The Eden Valley Walk follows, where possible, the course of the River Eden. The terrain is therefore fairly flat and along the Edenbridge section there are several Second World War pillboxes which stand guard along the river banks.

Edenbridge town is situated on the low-lying clays of the Low Weald which once were heavily wooded, rich in oak on the plain and with beech predominant on the Greensand Ridge to the north.

The close proximity of water brings a wealth of wildlife to the area including swans, herons, partridges and that elusive gem, the kingfisher.

Upper Eden Valley
Starborough Castle (2) (grid reference 426441) was built in the 1340s but destroyed on Cromwell's orders in 1650. Today, only the moat remains but an old picture, and evidence of the island, shows that it was originally as big as Bodiam, which can be visited in East Sussex.

The castle was surrounded by a medieval hunting park and Cernes Farm (3) (grid reference 425445) is situated on the northern boundary. It is a small medieval house, dating from about 1500, and has two bays - one of which formed an open hall. The house is timber-framed although tile hanging and brickwork have been used to repair

the ravages of time, a fate of many buildings which can be seen on the walk.

The footpath crosses an area of flat meadowland by the riverside (4) (grid reference 433449). This meadow formed an important part of the early agricultural scene. Winter flooding produced a good hay crop on the land and this was of sufficient importance for it to be held in common by various farms in the parish. Each held a strip of the field which they cut for hay before the end of July. On 1 August (Lammas Day) the meadow was thrown open for common grazing. Consequently some of the land is still known as Lammas land.

An apparent copse alongside the path conceals a 13th-century moated site known as Devils' Den (5) (grid reference 438452). It was probably a farmstead and fishing ground, although the original building no longer remains. The sinister name is one frequently given to earthworks of unknown origin.

The highest ground to the south is Dry Hill (6) (grid reference 433417), an area which probably supports the oldest historic site in the area. It is an early Iron Age fort, built around the 1st century BC. Local tribespeople, practising iron smelting, apparently retreated there in times of danger.

Looking towards higher ground to the east, a disused windmill is visible (7) (grid reference 445455). It is situated close to Edenbridge War Memorial Hospital and its 19th-century owners also owned the town's watermill. The windmill closed down in 1886 and the sails were later removed - but plans are now in progress to restore the feature and replace the cap and sweeps.

Edenbridge
Edenbridge High Street, once a Roman Road running from London to Lewes, grows in character towards the south. The original road was established to provide access to fertile corn-growing areas of the South Downs, and to create a

transport route for the local iron trade. The road owes its survival to the bridge (15) - it provided an essential crossing over a nameless river. Several bridges over the river have replaced the original, the second being built by Eadhelm. Edenbridge grew and prospered during the time of Eadhelm's bridge, resulting in both the town and river receiving their names.

There are many charming timbered buildings fronting the High Street. The route passes Church House (9) (circa 1400) and a lovely old barn (8) which now houses the Town Council. The nearby 14th-century Crown Hotel (10) has an unusual sign spanning the road. It is steeped in smuggling history and the 15th-century tap room was once the scene of secret drinking of illicit liquor.

Opposite, Taylor House (now Chevertons) (11) received its name from Sir William Taylour, Lord Mayor of London in 1469. The nearby watermill (14) is now a thriving restaurant. It is named 'Honours Mill' after the last working owners, and renovation, after its closure in 1969, included installing a sawn oak beam from the Hever Estate as a foundation for the machinery housing.

The town was once a local centre for the leather industry, having a thriving boot and shoe trade. Joseph Sparrowhawk, a local trader, is reputed to have regularly walked 29 miles (47 kilometres) to London and back. He carried finished boots and returned with leather. He eventually died in 1898, aged 86.

Edenbridge Church
The church (12) is dedicated to St Peter and St Paul and occupies the site of an earlier Saxon place of worship. It contains remains of a Norman window and was partially rebuilt in the 13th and 14th centuries, the tower being 13th century with a Perpendicular style spire. It has a most interesting feature - an unusual clock with just one hand! The aforementioned Sir William Taylour left

£6.13.4d. to the church when he died in 1483. It was donated for "The parish church of Edenbregg where I was christened".

The Eden Valley Walk enters and leaves Edenbridge town via a bridge crossing the railway line beyond the church. In fact, as a result of rivalry between railway building entrepreneurs, Edenbridge boasts two railway lines. The northernmost cross-country line was opened in 1842 for South Eastern Railway. The Town line (19) was opened for the London, Brighton and South Coast Railway in 1888, after many delays. It was then possible to catch a through train to Eastbourne.

Visible from the open farmland on the edge of Edenbridge is the large Tudor chimney stack of Skinners Farm (16) (grid reference 453467), a fine house dating from the 16th century. A distinct depression at an area known as Claypits (17) (grid reference 458465) reminds walkers that it was not so peaceful here during wartime. It was used as an anti-aircraft gun site and the enclosed area hides a Royal Observer Corps bunker.

Near the railway line, the path passes Delaware Farm (18) (grid reference 459458). It is situated on a probable moated site dating from the 13th century but the main house was built in 1679. Additional buildings date from the 15th to 17th centuries and the area has changed dramatically in more recent years with the division and sale of the original estate. There are now several converted farm buildings which form separate dwellings and the surrounding farmland has been divided and fenced.

People travel from far afield to visit Hever Castle and the church. But a single visit leaves little time to experience the pleasures of the surrounding countryside. Walkers, however, are able to appreciate both the natural history and the ancient

Crown Hotel, Edenbridge

landmarks of the area whilst walking through Hever Parish.

For instance, crossing the fields near Hever Station there are extensive views to Limpsfield Chart and the Greensand Ridge in the north and towards Dry Hill in the south-west across typical Wealden countryside. The route across the Hever estate is particularly enjoyable. It supports rich hedgerow plants including ladies bedstraw and meadow sweet; the latter was once used as an air freshener.

The area is a favourite hunting ground for kestrels, sparrowhawks and owls and, according to a vandalised sign near the railway, poisonous snakes! It warns of adders and ominously directs victims to Edenbridge Hospital.

Mid Eden Valley

Lydens Farm (20) (grid reference 458447) is a notable landmark. It is a four-bay hall house which dates from 1450, with an 18th-century brick frontage.

Hever Station (21) (grid reference 465445) was opened in 1888 on a branch of the London, Brighton and South Coast Railway. The peaceful scene was not so calm in the late 19th century when the Mark Beech Riots occurred, resulting in foreign workers being chased down the line of the railway to Edenbridge. Close to the station is St Nicholas Cottage (22) (grid reference 466443) which was once a public house.

The walk passes several attractive cottages including Chippens and Drive Cottage, dating back several hundred years. Nearby, Chippens Bank House (23) (grid reference 470446) was formerly the home of a Miss Everest. Mount Everest was named after Sir

Footpath access to the route from Lingfield

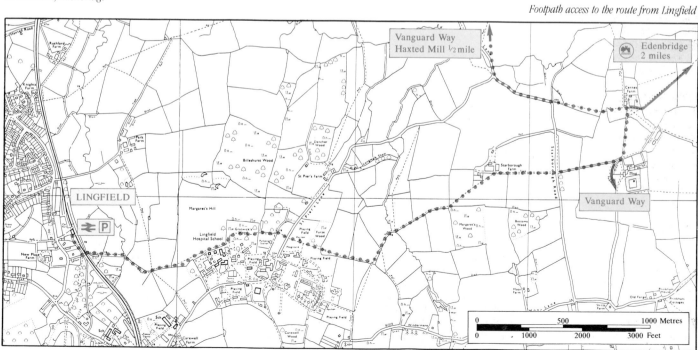

George Everest, her father and Surveyor General to the Indian Government.

The oldest part of the impressive Hever Grange (24) (grid reference 472446) was originally known as Crouch House Farm and is believed to date back to the 14th century. The somewhat smaller thatched cottage in Hever Road is called South Bank (25) (grid reference 474448)and is typical of many such cottages which were once numerous in the area.

Walkers will be reminded of the historical connections in the village when they reach Henry VIII Public House (26) (grid reference 476448). It was known as the 'Bull and Butcher' until 1830 and it is naturally a popular stop for visitors.

Hever Castle

This famous landmark (28) (grid reference 478452) dates back over 700 years. It was a small fortified farmhouse with moat and wooden drawbridge, subsequently rebuilt in 1462 by the Bullens. Each of Thomas Bullen's children left their name in our history books. Anne Bullen (or Boleyn) became King Henry VIII's second wife, mother to the future Queen Elizabeth I. She was eventually beheaded for committing an alleged incestuous relationship with her brother, George. Mary became Henry's mistress.

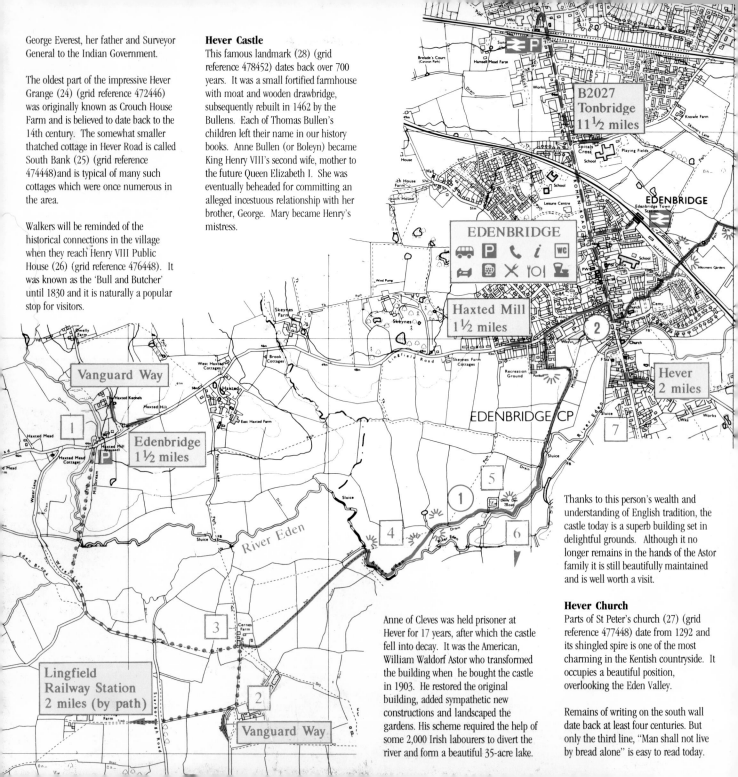

Thanks to this person's wealth and understanding of English tradition, the castle today is a superb building set in delightful grounds. Although it no longer remains in the hands of the Astor family it is still beautifully maintained and is well worth a visit.

Hever Church

Parts of St Peter's church (27) (grid reference 477448) date from 1292 and its shingled spire is one of the most charming in the Kentish countryside. It occupies a beautiful position, overlooking the Eden Valley.

Remains of writing on the south wall date back at least four centuries. But only the third line, "Man shall not live by bread alone" is easy to read today.

Anne of Cleves was held prisoner at Hever for 17 years, after which the castle fell into decay. It was the American, William Waldorf Astor who transformed the building when he bought the castle in 1903. He restored the original building, added sympathetic new constructions and landscaped the gardens. His scheme required the help of some 2,000 Irish labourers to divert the river and form a beautiful 35-acre lake.

Within the church is the tomb of Sir Thomas Bullen, together with much admired brasses. They include one of Sir Thomas in the robes of a Knight of the Garter.

Until recent years this pretty church upheld an annual custom of blessing the fields on Rogation Sunday in May.

FEATURES OF INTEREST

1. **Haxted Mill**
   Built about 1580 on early 14th-century foundations, with additions in 1794, the watermill has been restored to full working order.

2. **Starborough Castle**
   This castle, built in the 1340s, was destroyed on Cromwell's orders in about 1650. Today, only the moat remains.

3. **Cernes Farm**
   A small timber-framed house dating from 1500 with later tile-hanging and brickwork.

4. **Flat Meadow**
   This area was one-time held in common by farms for haymaking and later in the year used for common grazing.

5. **Devils' Den**
   There are no visible remains of a farmstead which probably existed on this 13th-century moated site.

6. **Dry Hill**
   An early Iron Age fort, built around the 1st century BC, to which local tribespeople retreated in times of danger.

7. **Windmill**
   This mill was in use until 1886 when it was closed and the sails removed.

8. **Doggetts Barn and**
   & **Church House**
9. Originally called Doggetts Farm, these half-timbered buildings date from 1400. The former now houses the Edenbridge Town Council Chamber and Offices.

10. **Crown Hotel**
    This 15th-century inn, which has a sign spanning the road, is steeped in smuggling history.

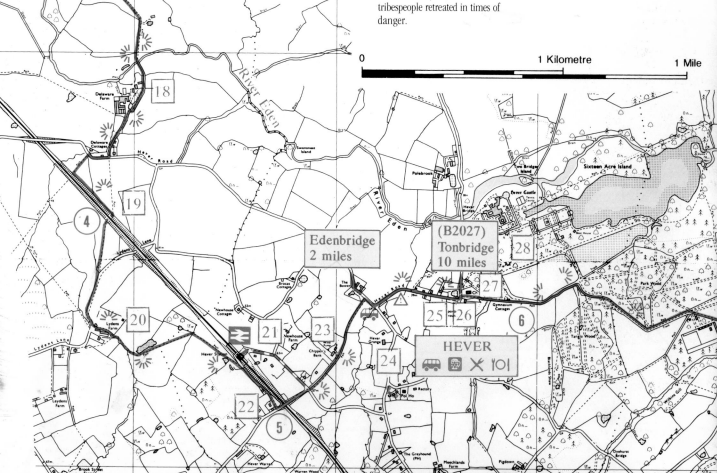

11. Taylor House

A timber-framed house named after Sir William Taylour, Lord Mayor of London in 1469.

12. Church of St Peter and St Paul, Edenbridge

Occupying the site of an earlier Saxon church, it dates from the Norman period with later medieval work.

13. Tanyard House

Behind the 15th-century house was a notable late 19th-century weather-boarded tanning shed on brick piers.

14. Watermill

Named 'Honour's Mill' after the last owner of the working mill, it was closed in 1969 and became a restaurant.

15. Bridge

The present sandstone bridge, dated 1834, replaced several earlier bridges on this important river crossing.

16. Skinners Farm

Dating from the 16th century, the main house is noted for a large Tudor chimney stack.

17. Claypits

An area where there is a large depression which was the location of a wartime anti-aircraft gun.

18. Delaware Farm

A feature of the farmhouse built in 1679, is a shell hood over the door. The original farm probably occupied a moated site.

19. Railway

This branch line was built in the 1880s for the London, Brighton and South Coast Railway.

20. Lydens Farm

Dating from 1450, the four-bay hall house has an 18th-century brick frontage.

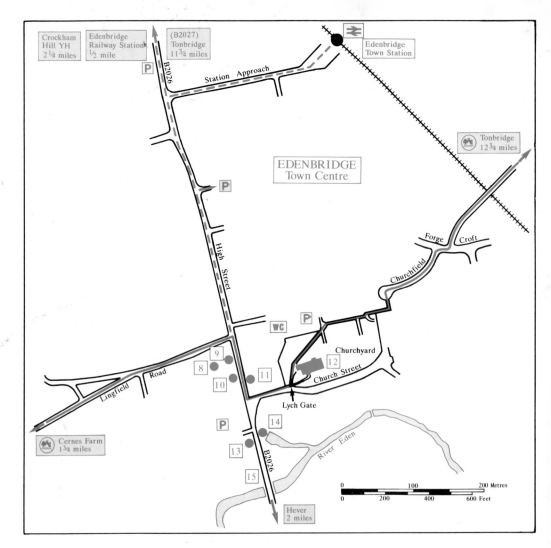

21. Hever Station

Opened in 1888, the station was the scene of the Mark Beech Riots in the 19th century.

22. St Nicholas Cottage

The festively named cottage alongside the railway was once a public house.

23. Chippens Bank House

Formerly the home of a Miss Everest. Mount Everest was named after Sir George Everest, her father.

24. Hever Grange

Dating back to the 14th century, the oldest part of the house was known as Crouch House Farm.

25. South Bank

A small thatched cottage built in the vernacular style of architecture

26. Henry VIII Public House

This attractive inn with its historical connections was, until 1830, known as 'The Bull and Butcher'.

27. St Peter's Church, Hever

Dating from 1292, its 14th century tower supports a shingle spire. Inside is a brass to Sir Thomas Bullen.

28. Hever Castle

A 13th century moated castle, the birthplace of Anne Boleyn, and restored by William Waldorf Astor in 1903.

St Peter's Church and lych-gate, Hever

2

**Threshers Field (Hever) –
Haysden Water
6 miles, allow 3 hours**

*The Parish of Chiddingstone
includes a hamlet, Hill Hoath,
the western access to which is
through a gorge of Hastings
sandstone. It is a sedimentary
deltaic deposit of the shallow
waters of Cretaceous times and
indications of quarrying are
apparent.*

*Hill Hoath consists of a small
group of houses and the area
offers attractive walking with
good views of Chiddingstone
Castle to the north. There is
still much evidence of the gale
damage from the 1987 storm
but existing woodland
provides a habitat for a wide
variety of wildlife. Mistletoe
growing on the upper branches
of trees is visible from the
road.*

*The footpath leading to
Chiddingstone is nearby and it
is a short diversion which is
well worth taking. The pretty
village is owned by the
National Trust.*

Lower Eden Valley

Near Threshers Field, the footpath
crosses a substantial brick and Hastings
sandstone bridge (29) (grid reference
492447) which might suggest that the
route was once more significant.
Further clues to the history of the area
are to be found at the site of Highfield
House, or the Dower House (30) (grid
reference 494445). A cleared area at the
site with daffodils and nettles growing,
shows evidence of occupation.

References to Heghefield in the Rent
Resolute of Chidyngston Burghershe
Manor in 1383 probably refer to the
former property here. During the 18th
century it was owned by the Streatfeilds
and later by the estate until the
building's demise after the Second World
War.

Hill Hoath (31) (grid reference 498446)
was once called both Willetts and
Knights, reflecting the occupation of
resident families. During the 17th and
18th centuries it housed a cooper,
tanner, blacksmith and shoemaker at
varying times, but not, apparently, a
candlestick maker!

Walkers will notice 'Withers' (32) (grid
reference 497447), a 15th-century
timber-framed hall house which has a
prominent Tudor chimney stack and a
hipped roof. It once housed the village
laundry. To the south-east is a fine barn
(33) (grid reference 499446) which has
five bays and double doors on both sides
of a single threshing floor. The doors
face east and west, allowing threshing
and winnowing to be assisted by the
wind. There is evidence that the original
structure may have been 15th century,
though most of the existing building is
probably 17th century – the size
indicating prosperity.

Chiddingstone Village

The village spans over 600 years of
history and has been beautifully
preserved by the National Trust. The
row of Kentish houses, shop, public
house and church is probably one of the
most photographed and sketched scenes
in the country.

The buildings date from the 14th and
15th centuries and there has been a
village shop on the present site since the
16th century. The Castle Inn (36) (grid
reference 501451) is the relatively recent
name for an inn which occupied this site
in 1420. It was known as Waterslip
House, then Rock House, the Bell and
finally the Five Bells.

Chiddingstone had a church and a
village street at the time the Domesday
Book was compiled – the earliest
documented record is to be found in
Rochester – naming 'Chidingstone' in
the 11th century.

There are many tales of ghosts in the
village. But a story of a cavalier who
climbed the church tower at midnight
was recently discounted by a verger who
revealed that he regularly climbed to
wind the old church clock! There is,
apparently, a headless coachman who
occasionally drives through the village,
using the old coach road. The High
Street has been used as a film set in
recent years, including 'Elizabeth I',
starring Glenda Jackson and 'Room with
a View'. The entire row of buildings is
now in the hands of the National Trust.

Chiding Stone

The Chiding Stone (35) (grid reference
501451) which is a large boulder of
Ardingly sandstone and reached by a
footpath from the village street, is one of
the alleged origins of the village's name.
There are many myths surrounding the
stone – it is said that one of the wayward
village wives was taken there for a public
scolding. But others say that the stone
was used as a platform from which the
preacher could guide his followers, in
the days before the church existed, over
1,000 years ago.

Chiddingstone Church

St Mary's Church (37) (grid reference
501452) has an amusing feature set
high on the west tower – a collection of
strange stone faces, some of which are
putting out their tongues in a derisory
gesture towards the village.

It is a beautiful building constructed mainly from local sandstone and it is steeped in history. The earliest identifiable masonry is found in rubble facing on the east wall of the chancel where there are remains of 13th-century Early English triple lancet windows. In the early 1600s, lightning struck, causing extensive fire damage. It was rebuilt between 1625 and 1629 and fire-marked stones can still be seen in places today.

Chiddingstone Castle

The Castle (34) (grid reference 498451) was built as a Tudor house and later demolished to make way for a 17th-century brick mansion. For centuries this home of the Streatfeild family was known as High Street House. However, much elaborate stonework was used to encase the manor house towards the end of the 18th century and the Gothic appearance, which incorporated towers, turrets and battlements, led to a change of name.

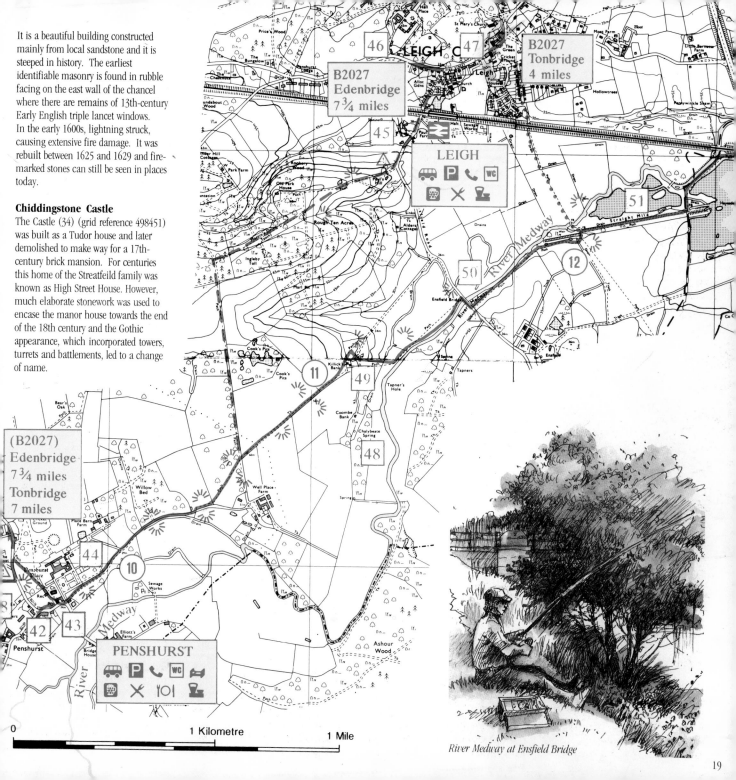

River Medway at Ensfield Bridge

Penshurst Churchyard

This manorial estate once included the entire village within its boundaries but, upon the death of Sir Henry Streatfeild in 1936, the castle was sold becoming a school and later was occupied by the army. In 1955, Chiddingstone was sold to Mr Denys Eyre Bowen, a gentleman who claimed Stuart blood. The building housed his collection of Japanese armour and Stuart portraits including a nude painting of Nell Gwynne.

Resuming the Eden Valley Walk, the route follows the old coach road (38). In documents and on estate maps the road was frequently referred to as Court Green Lane. It is thought that Court Green refers to the 'Forlese' of the Manor of Chidyngston Burghershe, of which the moated site remains are hidden in trees alongside the stream to the north. Evidence of hop gardens can still be seen, and along the track near Wat Stock, remains of a kiln (39) (grid reference 507439) used for preparing hop poles, still exists.

Next to the old coach road is Wat Stock Farm (40) (grid reference 507439). The original 15th-century house is a fine half-timbered example, it is timber-framed and has a hipped roof and Tudor chimney. It is now partially hidden behind farm buildings.

The views along the route here are probably some of the finest in the area - from Gillridge promontory (41) looking north across the Eden Valley. The landscape takes in the Low Weald, Greensand Ridge and North Downs.

A walk through the Penshurst Parish offers far reaching views across beautiful countryside. In Penshurst itself there is a bridge over the Eden, where the river bank is a mass of flowering plants in summer. A short distance downstream the Eden joins the Medway and the swelling river wends its way towards Tonbridge.

Many walkers will wish to linger awhile in the village, particularly at the church. The mansion, Penshurst Place, deserves a separate visit. From the footpath through its ancient park the walker has a fine view of the west front of the house.

Walkers enter or leave the parish on the old coach road which has wide ditches on each side. It is easy to imagine it being used in former times when it linked Penshurst with Chiddingstone, Hever and Edenbridge. A bridge crosses the Eden at a popular spot for fishing (grid reference 521438) and the path emerges one hundred yards to the north of Penshurst Village.

Penshurst Village
Sited on rising ground above the river which is liable to flooding, Penshurst contains an attractive group of houses with a fine medieval church with its adjoining rectory.

The walker approaches the Church of St John the Baptist through an enclosure known as Leicester Square (42) (grid reference 527438) surrounded on three sides by houses dating from the 16th century and named after Robert Sidney, Earl of Leicester, who owned, as well, London's famous Leicester Square.

Penshurst Church
This beautiful church (43) (grid reference 527439) dates from the 12th century. Its massive medieval tower, of local sandstone, dominates the village. Thomas Becket, martyred in 1170, appointed the first clerk in charge of the church before his death. His memory lives on in the beautiful 'Becket Window' of stained glass designed by the well known artist Lawrence Lee, himself a Penshurst resident. It depicts Becket standing before Penshurst Church and includes a mention of the ancient Church of Saint Jacques in Mont-Saint-Aignan, now Edenbridge's twin town. Becket visited the French town in 1135 and in 1970 Penshurst Parish formed a link as part of its commemoration of a long Christian history.

At the south-east end of the church, adjoining the chancel is the family chapel of the Sidneys where members of the family are commemorated from the 16th century to the present day. Other noteworthy features include the 'Smiling Lady' in the tower and the Luke Tapestry over the side altar.

The beautiful rectory with its Queen Anne elevation of red brick was formed out of a medieval tithe barn.

Penshurst Place
The origins of this impressive house (44) (grid reference 528440) are not precisely recorded. The earliest part may date from the 13th or even the 12th century. Its splendour was established when the merchant banker, Sir John de Pulteney, acquired the manor from its previous owners in 1338.

The still complete 14th-century manor house, at the centre of the building, is Pulteney's. Its most outstanding feature is the Great Hall, as it still stands unaltered after some 650 years. In the following century, in around 1420, the house was purchased by John, Duke of Bedford, brother of Henry V. Three generations of the Stafford family, the Dukes of Buckingham, owned Penshurst between 1447 and 1521. The last Duke was beheaded and the house and estate became royal property.

In 1552 King Edward VI gave the house and estate to Sir William Sidney for his faithful service to the King and his predecessors.

Sir William's son, Sir Henry Sidney, extended the house. Despite later alterations Penshurst, as it now stands, follows the plan established in Queen Elizabeth I's reign. Sir Henry Sidney's son, the famous Sir Philip, poet, statesman and soldier, was born at Penshurst in 1554. The present owner, William Sidney, Viscount De L'Isle, VC, KG, succeeded to Penshurst in 1945.

The extensive walled gardens represent the creations of the 16th and 17th centuries. The formality in design which has been the distinguishing feature of the gardens from the beginning has been preserved, but relaid with plants and shrubs which modern horticulture has introduced.

Penshurst Place receives many thousands of visitors every year and it is recognised as one of the greatest houses in Kent.

Part of the walk between Penshurst and Leigh is within the boundary of the Penshurst Park Plantation and it is necessary to keep dogs on leads.

Walkers pass walled gardens with neatly trimmed hedges above the old brick boundary. This ancient wall of Penshurst Place is home to barren strawberry, pellitory-of-the-wall, and ivy-leaved toadflax, the latter of which was once alien to Britain but now widespread in locations of this nature.

The fence posts near Well Place are coloured a dull green due to a powdery lichen called lecanora conizaeoides. It is a sign of the times as it once was rare in Britain but has spread rapidly with the increase in atmospheric pollution.

In the high branches of tall trees which can be seen from the path are several rookeries. Two newly formed ponds play host to mute swans and Canada geese despite the fact that there is yet little vegetation around their margins.

From a point near the top of the hill there is a good view of Tonbridge, with the spire of St Stephen's church clearly visible.

The woodland itself is mixed, containing mature oak, ash and hazel, and is home for a large number of birds including tree creepers and long-tailed tits. There is evidence of recent coppicing in the area, a practice of growing a small area of trees for periodic cutting.

View towards Penshurst Place from the north-east

Upper Medway Valley

The spur to and from Leigh passes very few houses as it crosses park and woodland, but near the railway is situated Paul's Farm (45) (grid reference 544461). The name of the farm derives from the de Polle family who were resident in the Tonbridge area in the 13th century. In 1307 William de Polle bought Paul's Farm from Ralph de Chaney of Hall Place. By the 15th century the family had left the building and migrated to the Detling area, becoming known as Polle of the Hill - or Polhill. They gave their name to the turnpike road built up the North Downs, now known as Polhill. Paul's Farmhouse is a listed building which dates from 16th century or earlier.

Leigh Village

Pronounced 'Lye', the village was originally spelt 'Lyghe' and was an ancient deer park until the 16th century. Although much of the settlement has an Elizabethan or Tudor appearance, it was actually built around 1876.

Leigh has gradually expanded over the years but it contains many relics of the historical past. The manor house, Hall Place, was the work of George Devey, as was the village hall and the water pumping station. The latter was built in order to provide fresh water for the estate workers in the village. Several impressive gatehouses guard the entrance to Hall Place and opposite the walls of the estate in the High Street is an attractive row of cottages. Leigh has a large village green and a thriving cricket team.

Leigh Church

St Mary's Church (47) (grid reference 549466) dates from the 13th century and has 14th and 16th-century features. The tower and most of the walls were rebuilt in 1802. It occupies a picturesque position adjacent to the village green.

Hall Place

Once called Leigh Hall, Hall Place (46) (grid reference 544466) is now owned by Lord Hollenden. The manor dates from Elizabethan times and is built of traditional red brick.

The grounds of the building are often open to the public and they attract many visitors. Within are exotic trees and shrubs which are carefully labelled for all to enjoy. These include fine examples of ginkgo, tulip, magnolia and strawberry trees.

Railway

The Tonbridge to Redhill line (53), built by the South Eastern Railway Company, was the original route from London to the Channel ports (Folkestone and Dover). Work commenced in November 1837 and the line opened between Redhill and Tonbridge (then spelt Tunbridge) on 31 May 1842. Edenbridge station opened with the completion of the line, Penshurst and Leigh several years later. The line was completed to Folkestone in June 1843 and to Dover in February 1844. The railway celebrates its 150th anniversary in 1992.

On the main route, the Eden Valley Walk passes nearby the Chalybeate spring (48) (grid reference 543446). It is similar to those at the famous Tunbridge Wells spa - being a natural mineral water spring which is impregnated with iron salts. People once travelled many miles to visit these health-giving spas in order to partake of their invigorating and healing properties.

The path passes Killick's Bank (49) (grid reference 542450), a late medieval hall house which may well be the earliest house in the parish. It is said that Lady Yonge, who inherited one half of the Penshurst Estate in 1758, had a detailed map made of her land. This shows 'Little Farm' on the site of Killick's Bank. Thomas Killick and his family

Oast-house near Gillridge Promontory

seem to have been tenants at the farm in the early part of the 19th century and they apparently gave their name to the dwelling.

Ensfield Bridge (50) (grid reference 547453) was so named after the Manor of Ensfield was granted to Sir William Sidney together with the Manor of Penshurst. The 18th-century farmhouse was pulled down some years ago. The road from Leigh to Ensfield first appeared on the 1801 Ordnance map. The present bridge, which replaced an earlier one, was built about 1940.

FEATURES OF INTEREST

29. **Bridge**
A substantial brick and Hastings sandstone bridge believed to carry the important route of the old coach road.

30. **Highfield House**
The site of the Dower House owned by the Streatfeilds during the 18th century, then later by Hever Castle until its demise.

31. **Hill Hoath**
An old settlement which during the 17th and 18th centuries housed variously a cooper, tanner, blacksmith and shoemaker.

32. **'Withers'**
A one-time laundry, this 15th-century timber-framed hall house possesses a Tudor chimney-stack and hipped roof.

33. Barn
Dating from the 15th century, this five-bayed structure was incorporated into a 17th-century addition.

34. Chiddingstone Castle
Originally known as High Street House, the manor house was remodelled into a castellated mansion in the 19th century.

35. Chiding Stone
Many myths surround this large sandstone boulder which is one of the alleged origins of the village's name.

36. Castle Inn
Dated 1637, and noted for its pargeting, it forms part of a row of 16th and 17th-century timber-framed buildings.

37. St Mary's Church, Chiddingstone
This 14th-century church was largely rebuilt after a fire in 1625. Prominent are the pinnacles surmounting the tower.

38. Coach Road
The old coach road was probably used in former times as a carriage road between Hever and Penshurst.

39. Kiln
The remains of a kiln used for preparing hop poles.

40. Wat Stock Farm
Obscured by farm buildings is a 15th-century half-timbered house with hipped roof and Tudor chimney.

41. Gillridge Promontory
From the ridge are excellent views to the north across the Eden Valley.

42. Leicester Square
A group of cottages forming the entrance to the churchyard and named after the Elizabethan, Earl of Leicester.

43. Church of St John the Baptist, Penshurst
The interior dates from the 13th century. Except for the Perpendicular tower, the exterior is 19th century.

44. Penshurst Place
An outstanding example of a complete 14th-century manor house with its fine medieval great hall and later additions.

45. Paul's Farm
A listed 16th-century timber-framed and weather-boarded house on the site of an earlier building.

46. Hall Place
The mansion dates from 1871-6 and built in the Tudor style with red-brick and blue diapering, and sandstone dressings.

47. St Mary's Church, Leigh
Dating back to the 13th century, the church was not finally completed until 1862.

48. Chalybeate Spring
Near Well Place Farm is a spring of water impregnated with iron salts.

49. Killick's Bank
A late medieval hall house and arguably the oldest house in the parish of Leigh.

50. Ensfield Bridge
The present bridge, which replaced an earlier one, was built in about 1940.

51. Straight Mile and Long Reach
Parts of a canal which were dug in 1829 for the Penshurst Canal Company, but never completed.

3

**Haysden Water - Tonbridge
2 miles, allow 1 hours**

A portion of this stretch of the Eden Valley Walk passes through the attractive Haysden Country Park. The route follows the River Medway closely and there is much wildlife to be seen in the area.

Haysden Country Park
This Country Park (58) occupies some 165 acres of the Medway Valley to the west of Tonbridge. It stretches from the urban edge (Barden) at its eastern end to the borough boundary immediately west of Haysden Water. The River Medway runs the length of its northern boundary and is crossed by Lucifer Bridge which gives access to Barden Lake.

The park occupies former pastureland and the landscape has changed considerably since the early 19th century. This is largely due to the successive influences of transport developments, river management and gravel extraction.

Tonbridge and Malling Borough Council made land acquisition and access arrangements during the 1980s. The park development provided an interesting, informal recreational area with easy access to the town, and protected valuable wildlife habitats. The most obvious features of the park today are two lakes, Haysden Water (52) (grid reference 561458) and Barden Lake (61) (grid reference 575462). They result from gravel extraction in the 1970s and are popular for fishing and other water sports.

Haysden Water in Haysden Country Park

But changes to the original grazing meadows started in the late 1820s when James Christie, an entrepreneur, set out to challenge the monopoly of the existing Medway Navigation Company. He planned to extract valuable oak timber at Penshurst and carry it downstream in barges. A letter to the press at the time gives a clue that Christie envisaged a canal to Forest Row and thence to the river Arun, and on to Portsmouth.

He constructed a lock, known as 'Stone Lock' (59) (grid reference 571461) which can still be seen to the south of the bend in the main new River Medway channel. He also created a canal, known as the 'Straight Mile' (51). Part of this is now used as a bridleway within the park. The Straight Mile canal was never used, but it remained as a dry channel across the site of the Flood Relief Barrier, through Haysden Water and beyond.

James Christie disappeared, reputedly to Canada, before his scheme was completed. But transport developments were rapid and in 1842 the Edenbridge - Tonbridge rail line (53) was completed, giving access to London.

The A21 Tonbridge bypass (54), which dominates the skyline at the western end of the park was opened in 1970 by the then Prime Minister, Edward Heath. The viaduct is over $\frac{1}{4}$" mile long and it spans about half the natural valley, the rest being crossed by an embankment.

The Flood Relief Barrier (55) (grid reference 564461), which crosses the park north to south, was constructed in 1979/80, to control the flow of water through Tonbridge at times of high rainfall. The whole of the Haysden Water area of the park can be flooded to within a few feet of the top of the barrier, and the area of water impounded can stretch to 686 acres. The last major flooding incident in Tonbridge was in 1968. In conjunction with the construction of the barrier and the control gates the river was diverted from its original course, through the meandering shallows, down the straight new River Medway channel.

The newly planted 'Heusenstaam Friendship Wood' (56) (grid reference 565461), just downstream of the control gates, marks Tonbridge's association with its German twin town, and the devastation of the 1987 Great Storm. The wood is on the site of the old brick weir and pools along the original river course, which was once a playground for generations of Tonbridge children. Part of 'The Shallows' (57) (grid reference 568459), as the area was known, can still be seen to the south of the railway, near the main car park.

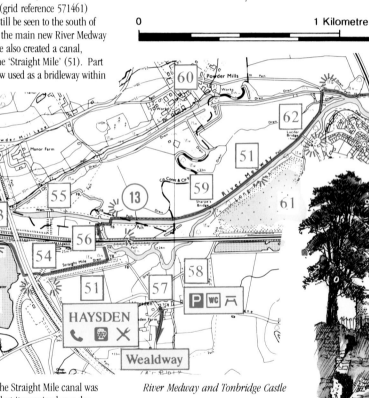

River Medway and Tonbridge Castle

The River Medway is well-known for kingfishers, and the varied habitats in the park support a wide range of wildlife including butterflies, dragonflies, water plants, native hedge and tree species and a range of resident and migrating birds. On Haysden Water can be seen herons, Canada and greylag geese, coot, moorhens, great crested grebe, and mallard and sometimes in this area, a kestrel hovering.

To the north, the dark buildings on the skyline visible between trees from the new River Medway channel towpath, mark the site of the former gunpowder works, known as the 'Powder Mills' (60) (grid reference 570467). The present buildings are used for chemical manufacture.

There is a lovely story behind the naming of the Lucifer Bridge (62) (grid reference 576465) over the River Medway at Barden. In the early 19th century this stretch of the river was straightened for the transportation of timber. The landowner of the surrounding land objected to the local people skating and boating on the river, so he erected a series of barriers. Battle was joined and the barriers were systematically removed. As a result a local wag wrote on the bridge 'How art thou fallen from heaven, O Lucifer' (Isaiah 15, v 12). The town laughed, the landowner did not try to block the river again and the name stuck. The old bridge was replaced by a steel one in 1896.

Tonbridge

In 1824 William Cobbett described Tonbridge as "a small but very nice town, with some fine meadows and a navigable river". The description is still apt today. The name 'Tonbridge' derives from the Saxon 'Dun' and 'Burgh' (hill fort), which probably refers to Castle Hill (Iron Age), south of the town. The town owes its existence to the crossing point of the Medway, which branches just upstream, and the castle that was built to protect it.

The Castle

The Castle Mound (67) (grid reference 589466) was built by the Normans on the site of a Saxon fort. The gatehouse, considered one of the finest examples in the country, and the walls, which remain to this day, are 13th century.

In addition to the vast curtain walls which enclosed the bailey area of the castle, the town was further defended by an outer town wall (71) of timber or stone and a fosse (or ditch). Permission to build this was given to the then owner of the castle, Richard de Clare, by Henry III. Traces of the Fosse survive in the gardens of the Cedars in Bordyke ('burgh dyke'), and the Hermitage, Lyons and Port Reeve in East Street. The Port Reeve's house (70) regulated entry on foot across the fosse from the east. Nothing remains of the outer wall today but it is possible that the stonework in the lower part of the Port Reeve's house is either stone from the wall or from the dismantled castle walls.

Following dismantling during the Civil War (1646), the Castle became a domestic residence. Both it and the grounds went into public ownership in 1897 and it now houses council offices, including the Tourist Information Centre.

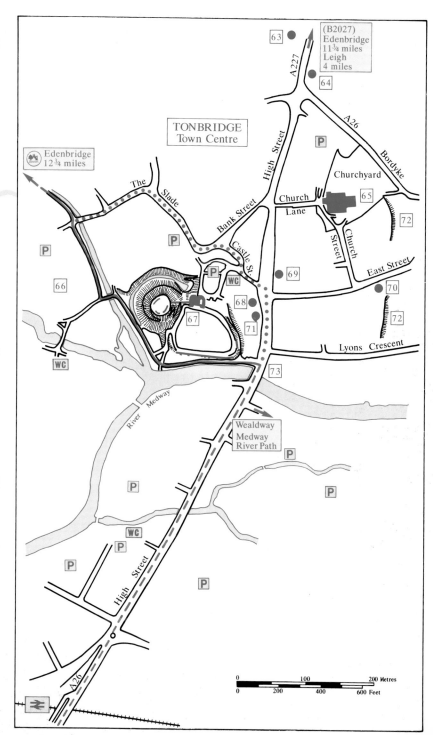

The Bridge

Henry VIII paid for a 'Great Bridge' (73) (grid reference 590465) across the river. The town was always important as an administrative and route centre, and during the 14th century tolls were levied on most commodities. These included grain, cattle, skins, timber, food, charcoal and nails.

The Town

By the mid 17th century the 'Chequers' (68) and the 'Rose and Crown' (69) were catering for travellers to the Chalybeate springs of 'The Wells' (now Tunbridge Wells) at what was then the southern tip of the parish.

The town has been known for the manufacture of Tunbridge Ware (decorated wood), gunpowder and cricket balls, and for tanning and printing. It was a nursery for many pre-war Kent cricketers, the site of the Angel Cricket Ground now being occupied by a leisure centre (the Angel Centre) and supermarket. The tradition of producing cricketers has been continued by Tonbridge School in the High Street.

FEATURES OF INTEREST

52. Haysden Water and
& Barden Lake
61. Within Haysden Country Park, the two lakes result from gravel extractions in the 1970s. They are popular for fishing and other water sports.

53. Railway
The Tonbridge to Redhill line, built in 1842 for the South Eastern Railway, celebrates its 150-year anniversary in 1992.

54. Tonbridge Bypass
The bypass (A21), which was opened in 1970 by Edward Heath, crosses the valley on a $1/4$" mile long viaduct.

55. Flood Relief Barrier
Constructed in 1979/80, the barrier controls the flow of water through Tonbridge at times of high rainfall.

Gatehouse, Tonbridge Castle

56. Heusenstamm Friendship Wood
The wood marks Tonbridge's association with its German twin town and the devastation of the great storm in 1987.

57. 'The Shallows'
The meanders of the original River Medway before it was diverted down the new channel when the Flood Relief Barrier was constructed.

58. Haysden Country Park
Haysden's main features are Barden Lake and Haysden Water. Provision is made for informal recreation and the protection of wildlife habitats.

59. Stone Lock
A lock constructed by James Christie in the late 1820s in connection with the unsuccessful scheme for the Penshurst Canal.

60. Powder Mills
On the site of a former gunpowder works are now buildings used for chemical manufacture.

62. Lucifer Bridge
Named from the biblical quotation : 'How art thou fallen from heaven, O Lucifer' following the landowners abortive attempt to stop skating and boating on the river.

63. Tonbridge School
The school, founded in 1553 by Sir Andrew Judde, was rebuilt in Victorian gothic style in the 19th century.

64. Ferox Hall
A Georgian house dating from 1755, with a stately front but Victorianised behind.

65. Church of St Peter and St Paul, Tonbridge
Built of sandstone, the church dates from the 12th century and was restored by Christian in 1877-9.

66. Miniature Railway
Constructed by Tonbridge Model Engineering Society, the miniature railway operates on fine summer weekends.

67. Tonbridge Castle
Remains of a large Norman motte and bailey castle with a 13th-century gatehouse originally containing a great hall.

68. Moss Bros and the
& 'Chequers'
71. Two fine and large 15th-century half-timbered gabled houses. The gables on the 'Chequers' have cusped bargeboards.

69. Rose and Crown Hotel
This 16th-century hotel has an 18th-century chequered brick front and a porch which spans the pavement.

70. Port Reeve's House
Originally a 16th-century half-timbered house, though now much altered. Notable are the oriel windows on brackets.

72. Town Wall
The remaining earthworks of a ditch associated with an outer town wall of timber or stone erected in the 13th century.

73. Bridge
The first stone bridge was built soon after the Norman invasion and later, Henry VIII paid for a 'Great Bridge'.

PLACES OF INTEREST TO VISIT
on or near the Eden Valley Walk

Bough Beech Reservoir (Information Centre)
Winkhurst Green, Tonbridge
tel: Maidstone (0622) 753017

Caxton Tonbridge Waterways
The Big Bridge, Castle Walk, Tonbridge
tel: Tonbridge (0732) 456918

Chiddingstone Castle
Chiddingstone, Edenbridge
tel: Penshurst (0892) 870347

Chiding Stone
Chiddingstone, Edenbridge

Haxted Mill and Museum
Haxted Road, Edenbridge
tel: Edenbridge (0732) 862914

Haysden Country Park
Haysden, Tonbridge
tel: West Malling (0732) 844522

Hever Castle
Hever, Edenbridge
tel: Edenbridge (0732) 865224

Milne Museum
The Slade, off Castle Street, Tonbridge
tel: Tonbridge (0732) 364726

Miniature Railway
(Tonbridge Model Engineering Society)
Recreation Ground, The Slade, Tonbridge
tel: Tonbridge (0732) 361217

Penshurst Place
Penshurst, Tonbridge
tel: Penshurst (0892) 870307

Penshurst Vineyards
Grove Road, Penshurst, Tonbridge
tel: Penshurst (0892) 870255

Tonbridge Castle
High Street, Tonbridge
tel: Tonbridge (0732) 844522

If you have enjoyed this walk and would like to explore other waymarked walking routes in Kent, write for a publications price list to the Recreation Paths Officer, Planning Department, Kent County Council, Springfield, Maidstone, Kent ME14 2LX.

OTHER WALKING OPPORTUNITIES

Linked to the Eden Valley Walk are a number of linear and circular walks, as follows:

Wealdway
Wealdway is an 80-mile linear route from the Thames Estuary at Gravesend to the English Channel at Beachy Head. It crosses the North and South Downs and the Kent and Sussex Weald. Between Tonbridge and Haysden Country Park, along a stretch of the River Medway, it coincides with the Eden Valley Walk.
Publications:
'Wealdway' - Geoffrey King. Wealdway Steering Group, 11 Old London Road, Brighton, East Sussex BN1 8XR.
'Wealdway Accommodation and Transport Guide' - Wealdway Steering Group, as above.
'Guide to the Wealdway' - John H Mason. Constable & Co, 11 Orange Street, London WC2H 3EW.
'The Wealdway and the Vanguard Way' - Kev Reynolds. Cicerone Press, 2 Police Square, Milnthorpe, Cumbria.

Vanguard Way
Vanguard Way is a 63-mile linear route from the London suburbs at Croydon to the English Channel at Seaford. It crosses the North and South Downs and the Kent, Surrey and Sussex Weald. The route links with the Eden Valley Walk at Cernes Farm, near Edenbridge.
Publications:
'The Vanguard Way' - Vanguard Rambling Club, c/o 109 Selsdon Park Road, South Croydon, Surrey CR2 8JJ.
'The Wealdway and the Vanguard Way' - Kev Reynolds. Cicerone Press, 2 Police Square, Milnthorpe, Cumbria.

Medway River Path
The Medway River Project was established in 1988 to enhance public access, amenity and nature conservation along the River Medway. The project promotes local community action in caring for the countryside. The proposed continuous riverside path is open at present between Tonbridge and East Peckham, and between Wateringbury and Allington.
Publications:
'Towpath Walks' - Medway River Project, 3 Lock Cottages, Lock Lane, Sandling, Maidstone, Kent ME14 3AU, and Kent County Council Planning Department, Springfield, Maidstone, Kent ME14 2LX

Edenbridge Walks
A series of countryside walks ranging from 2 to 6 miles within the Low Weald area, a relatively flat pastoral landscape, but encompassing an interesting variety of natural features and archaeological remains.
Publications:
'Six Country Walks Around Edenbridge' and 'Six Longer Country Walks Around Edenbridge' Edenbridge Town Council, Doggetts Barn, High Street, Edenbridge, Kent TN8 5AR.

Tonbridge Walks
A series of urban and countryside walks between 1 and 7 miles in and around Tonbridge. The varied landscapes comprise the River Medway, fields, woods, hop gardens, orchards and historic buildings.
Publication:
'14 walks in and around Tonbridge' - The Tonbridge Civic Society, c/o 3 Derby Close, Hildenborough, Tonbridge, Kent

TABLE OF PERIODS

Mesolithic	8000-3000 BC
Neolithic	3000-1800 BC
Bronze Age	1800-550 BC
Iron Age	550 BC-AD 43
Roman	43-410
Saxon	410-1066
Norman	1066-1200
Early English	1200-1300
Decorated	1300-1370
Perpendicular	1370-1540
Tudor	1540-1558
Elizabethan	1558-1603
Jacobean	1603-1630
Stuart	1630-1702
Queen Anne	1702-1714
Georgian	1714-1810
Regency	1810-1837
Victorian	1837-1900
Edwardian	1900-1936

FURTHER READING

Further information and details about places and features of interest passed en route can be obtained in the following books:

'Aspects of Edenbridge' - various authors, published by Edenbridge Historical Society
'Discovering Chiddingstone' - E D Hardcastle, published by D and E Aitchison
'Edenbridge Guide Book', published by Forward Publicity Ltd
'Edenbridge - the Past in Pictures' - Alan Dell, published by Edenbridge Historical Society
'Hever Castle' - guide book published by Hever Castle Ltd
'Lingfield Heritage' - Peter Gray, published by Lingfield Parish Council
'Penshurst Place' - Viscount De L'Isle
'Portrait of the River Medway' - Roger Penn, published by Robert Hale Ltd
'The Book of Tonbridge' - Frank Chapman, published by Barracuda Books Ltd
'The Visitor's Guide to Kent' - Kev Reynolds, published by Moorland Publishing Co
'The Weald' - J W Wooldridge and F Goldring, published by Collins
'Tonbridge, a Pictorial History' - Ivan Green, published by Phillimore Co Ltd
'Tonbridge Guide Book'
'Weald of Kent and Sussex' - Sheila Kaye-Smith, published by Robert Hale Ltd
'Yesterday's Town : Tonbridge' - Frank Chapman, published by Barracuda Books Ltd
Church Guides from Edenbridge, Hever and Chiddingstone churches
Local History Section in Tonbridge Reference Library

COUNTRYSIDE ACCESS CHARTER

YOUR RIGHTS OF WAY ARE

Public footpaths - on foot only. Sometimes waymarked in yellow.
Bridleways - on foot, horseback and pedal cycle. Sometimes waymarked in blue.
Byways - (usually old roads), most 'Roads Used as Public Paths' and, of course, public roads - all traffic.
Use maps, signs and waymarks. Ordnance Survey Pathfinder and Landranger maps show most public rights of way.

ON RIGHTS OF WAY YOU CAN

Take a pram, pushchair or wheelchair if practicable.
Take a dog (on a lead or under close control).
Take a short route round an illegal obstruction or remove it sufficiently to get past.

YOU HAVE A RIGHT TO GO FOR RECREATION TO

Public parks and open spaces - on foot.
Most commons near older towns and cities - on foot and sometimes on horseback.
Private land where the owner has a formal agreement with the local authority.

IN ADDITION you can use by local or established custom or consent, but ask for advice if you are unsure.
Many areas of open country like moorland, fell and coastal areas, especially those of the National Trust, and some commons.
Some woods and forests, especially those owned by the Forestry Commission.
Country parks and picnic sites.
Most beaches.
Towpaths on canals and rivers.
Some private paths and tracks.
Consent sometimes extends to riding horses and pedal cycles.

FOR YOUR INFORMATION

County and metropolitan district councils and London boroughs maintain and record rights of way, and register commons and village greens.
Obstructions, dangerous animals, harassment and misleading signs on rights of way are illegal and you should report them to the council.
Paths across fields can be ploughed; they must normally be reinstated within two weeks.
Landowners can require you to leave land to which you have no right of access.
Motor vehicles are normally permitted only on roads, byways and some 'Roads Used as Public Paths'.
Follow any local bylaws.

AND, WHEREVER YOU GO, FOLLOW THE COUNTRY CODE

Enjoy the Countryside and respect its life and work.
Guard against all risk of fire.
Fasten all gates.
Keep your dogs under close control.
Keep to public paths across farmland.
Use gates and stiles to cross fences, hedges and walls.
Leave livestock, crops and machinery alone.
Take your litter home.
Help to keep all water clean.
Protect wildlife, plants and trees.
Take special care on country roads.
Make no unnecessary noise.

This Charter is for practical guidance in England and Wales only. Fuller advice is given in a free booklet 'Out in the country' available from:
Countryside Commission Publications Despatch Department,
19-23 Albert Road, Manchester M19 2EQ.

Published with kind permission of the Countryside Commission.